Original title:
Tropical Embrace

Copyright © 2025 Creative Arts Management OÜ
All rights reserved.

Author: Henry Beaumont
ISBN HARDBACK: 978-1-80581-503-7
ISBN PAPERBACK: 978-1-80581-030-8
ISBN EBOOK: 978-1-80581-503-7

Breathing Serenity's Air

In the sun-kissed shade I sip,
A coconut smile on my lip.
Palm trees dance to the breeze,
Whispers of laughter among the leaves.

Sandy toes and ice cream woes,
Seagulls swoop in silly shows.
Flip-flops clapping a merry beat,
Giggling crabs scurry on tiny feet.

A parrot squawks a cheeky tune,
Under the watchful eye of the moon.
Beach towels sprawled like laughable art,
Creative chaos, a sandy heart.

In this realm of sun and cheer,
Every moment, a ticklish peer.
A hammock sways, a sleepy grin,
In this paradise, all troubles thin.

Flutter of Tropical Dancers

In a skirt made of leaves,
They jiggle and sway,
Even the coconuts laugh,
At their wild cabaret.

A parrot joins in,
With whistles and squawks,
While the palm trees giggle,
At their silly frocks.

Beach balls bounce high,
Like they're part of the team,
The sand joins the dance,
In a sun-kissed dream.

As waves clap their hands,
In a watery cheer,
These dancers twirl round,
With no hint of fear.

Blush of the Setting Sun

The sun takes a bow,
In a peachy attire,
Waves blush and giggle,
As the sky catches fire.

Seagulls titter overhead,
Dropping fries from the sky,
The fish roll with laughter,
As they swim by and sigh.

Palm trees stretch out,
Like they're fixing their hair,
They sway to the rhythm,
With the breeze in the air.

While the beach-goers snack,
On their chips and their dips,
The sunset flirts hard,
With a wink and some flips.

Melodies of the Tropics

A ukulele strums,
With a cheerful twang,
While lizards do the cha-cha,
In a jungle where it sang.

Coconuts play drums,
As the crabs do a jig,
Even turtles join in,
Doing the limbo gig.

With melodies floating,
On a breeze made of cheer,
You can hear the parrots,
Singing loud and clear.

In this funky forest,
Where the vibes are so bright,
Every leap and each bound,
Turns the day into night.

Heart of the Sunlit Paradise

In a hammock of laughter,
Under skies made of blue,
The sun plays peekaboo,
With a wink and a hue.

Chillin' fellow sloths,
Make a grand parade,
With their slow-motion flair,
They've got it made!

The ducks wear sunglasses,
As they strut in a line,
While the fish throw confetti,
In a splashy design.

As the day fades away,
Into giggles and fun,
This warm-hearted place,
Is never outdone.

Jewel-Toned Horizons

Bright birds squawk as they fly,
Colors dance in the sky.
Coconut falls with a thud,
And I slip right in the mud.

Lizards wear shades, oh so cool,
Join me, they're nobody's fool.
Sunshine spills like lemonade,
On a hammock, I wade and fade.

Bliss Beneath the Thatched Roof

Under the shade, it's a snore fest,
But the drinks make it the best.
Parrots argue with a crab,
Who's the king? Oh, what a jab!

Flip-flops squeak on the floor,
Sand castles wait by the shore.
With piña coladas in hand,
We're the silliest in the land.

Laughter Echoes in the Lagoon

Diving in for a splash and cheer,
The fish giggle, they know we're here.
A mermaid waves, but she is shy,
Making bubbles dance and fly.

Giggling kids with mismatched socks,
Floating by in silly flocks.
In this water, all is wild,
Even the clam plays like a child.

Dappled Light on Ferns

Sunlight twinkles through the trees,
Dancing leaves tease gentle bees.
A coconut falls, a sudden thump,
Then someone trips with a loud bump.

Under the ferns all snug they lay,
A troupe of friends who just can't sway.
Laughter rings out, a cheerful sound,
As we roll 'round on the ground.

Solstice of the Heart

Beneath the sun, we dance and play,
Sipping coconuts, all night, all day.
Flip-flops slapping, laughter rings,
As monkeys join us, wearing bling.

Pinch me quick, am I awake?
This joy's so real, I can barely shake.
With bright umbrellas, drinks in hand,
We tell tall tales on golden sand.

Solace Beneath Coconut Boughs

Under palm leaves, we take a seat,
Listening to the cicadas beat.
A crab scuttles by, in tiny haste,
Cracking jokes, we share our taste.

The sun dips low, a fiery ball,
We take a moment, heed the call.
Coconuts fall with a comedic thump,
As we all giggle at the resounding bump.

A Symphony of Raindrops

Raindrops tickle on our noses,
Tropical downpour, like nature's roses.
We slip and slide, what a funny show,
In puddles we jump, letting worries go.

The thunder rumbles like a distant drum,
Sharing giggles while getting numb.
Every splash a note, a melody bright,
Dancing in water, oh what a sight!

Nature's Silken Tresses

Breezes whisper through the branches,
Tickling our hair in playful stances.
Lizards wear tiny, flashy hats,
While we laugh at surfboards and splats.

A breeze so warm, it gives us glee,
As we attempt a dance—whoops, oh me!
With every tumble, our hearts grow light,
Nature giggles too, what a delight!

Hidden Oasis

In a place where coconuts sway,
Loud parrots laugh all day.
A sunburnt tourist sings off-key,
While sipping juice beneath a tree.

Flip-flops flop as crabs all dance,
A seagull steals a sandwich chance.
Vacationers lose their cool,
While waves come in, a splashy duel.

Sunscreen slathered, lathered thick,
The beach ball's lost, oh what a trick!
With every giggle, mischief flows,
In this hideaway that humor knows.

Dancing Palms

Palm branches shimmy in the breeze,
Where sun hats fly like birds with ease.
Swaying to the rhythmic beat,
Of dodging waves and sandy feet.

A hula contest gone awry,
As Aunt May pins a grass skirt high.
Uncle Joe, the king of slips,
Attempts to dance, but takes a dip!

With every shimmy, laughter spreads,
As beach balls bounce off plenty of heads.
The palm trees giggle in delight,
While evening stars join in the night.

Warm Sands and Echoed Dreams

Where warm sands tickle toes in glee,
And surfboards crash like an angry spree.
A beach towel flies, a fashion scare,
As Grandma sunbathes in her chair.

Echoes of laughter swell and dive,
While kids compete to make the most alive.
Sandcastles wobble, then they fall,
The tide comes in, a merry brawl!

In every grain, a dream is spun,
As sunscreen's applied, and jokes are fun.
With nightfall's glow, it's time to toast,
To goofy moments we adore the most.

Lush Reverie

In gardens where the coconuts bloom,
And lizards plot to steal a room.
Frantic hedgehogs chase the sun,
While iguanas nap, oh what fun!

A hammock swings, but oh the twist,
As friends take turns to make a list.
From funniest moments to grand escapes,
Every story bends and reshapes.

With drinks in hand and jokes to share,
Laughter echoes through warm, salty air.
In lush reverie, let mischief rise,
A feast of fun beneath the skies!

A Drift of Blossoms

In the jungle, flowers flip and flop,
Bees wear sunglasses, never stop.
Parrots gossip, perched high up,
Sipping nectar from a tiny cup.

Lizards dance with mighty flair,
Skippity-hop without a care.
Coconuts chuckle, rolling by,
Underneath the sun-soaked sky.

Monkeys swing with goofy grins,
Playing tag on leafy twins.
The world's a stage, with noise and cheer,
Each blossom knows it's time to peer.

So gather 'round this quirky show,
With every laugh, let good vibes grow.
In this garden, smiles ignite,
A drift of blossoms, pure delight.

Soliloquy of the Sands

Oh, the grains that tickle toes,
Like tiny fairies, goodness knows.
Waves crash, but they're in on the joke,
Whispering secrets without a poke.

Castles rise, then tumble down,
A sandy kingdom, no royal crown.
Seagulls squawk in melodious glee,
Announcing brunch, come dine with me!

Beach umbrellas, like colorful hats,
Hide picnic snacks from rogue little rats.
Frolic in sun, till burnt and brown,
Silly hats will always clown.

In this soliloquy from the shore,
Life's a beach, let's laugh some more.
As tides recede, we dance and twirl,
In the sands, our joy unfurl.

Fables of the Tropic Moon

Nights alight with whirling stars,
Crabs in tuxedos, oh so bizarre!
Fireflies flicker, a flash mob's glow,
Chasing shadows, putting on a show.

The moon serves punch, a glowing delight,
As creatures mingle, from night till light.
Turtles tell tales of ocean's lore,
While iguanas dance on the sandy floor.

Cocktails made of coconut tease,
In laughter's grasp, life's but a breeze.
Lunchtime dances, with rhythm and sway,
The tropic tales, they light our way.

So gather 'round for stories grand,
From the depths of this sandy land.
Fables weave with joy and tune,
In laughter's arms, beneath the moon.

Canvas of Tropical Dreams

Palette of colors, splashes bright,
Palm trees sway in infectious delight.
Brush strokes giggle as they leap,
Creating scenes that twinkle and peep.

A canvas filled with laughter's hue,
Where dolphins dance and parrots coo.
Pineapple hats, a sight to behold,
Stories of warmth and madness unfold.

The waves strike chords, a melody sings,
As crabs put on their finest bling.
Sunshine splatters, paintbrushes engage,
This happy canvas, a lively stage.

In dreams we wander, free as the breeze,
Find joy in the dance of the leaves.
A canvas where fun is supreme,
In the heart of all quirky dreams.

Graceful Tides and Gentle Winds

Ocean waves dance with glee,
Crabs strut like they own the spree.
Seagulls squawk, what a delight,
Surfboards fly, oh what a sight!

Palm trees sway, doing the twist,
Who knew a breeze could be a tryst?
Sandy toes in laughter land,
Sunburned noses, oh so grand!

Cocktails mix like a goofy song,
Umbrellas bright, all day long.
Sharks in shades swim with flair,
Giggling dolphins, unaware!

Under the sun, everyone's a star,
Beach balls bounce, not going far.
With laughter loud and smiles wide,
Embrace the joy, the ocean's tide!

A Canvas of Nature's Love

Colors burst in the morning light,
Painted skies, what a delight!
Birds in bowties, chirping tunes,
Turtles dance with afternoon moons.

Flowers gossip in the breeze,
Bumblebees wear tiny keys.
Every bloom is quite the fashion,
Nature's show, full of passion!

Fruits are ripe, the juice flows free,
Bananas in hats, oh can't you see?
Mangoes roll and have a race,
Pineapples join without a trace!

In every corner, laughter sings,
Breezy strolls and silly flings.
Nature chuckles, wild and bright,
Colorful joy, a sheer delight!

Island Whispers

Whispers float on the evening tide,
Parrots gossip, all side by side.
Shells collect tales from the sea,
Mermaids giggle at the glee!

Umbrellas twirl in a goofy dance,
Cockatoos join, lost in a trance.
Sandcastles with mustache crowns,
Waves cheering in joyful sounds!

Pineapple hats are all the rage,
Lemons laugh, caught in a stage.
Coconut drinks where fun abounds,
Laughter echoes, the best of sounds!

Stars peek out, a brilliant sight,
Fireflies spark with sheer delight.
Together we whirl on this blissful shore,
Island whispers, forevermore!

Sun-Kissed Serenade

Sunrise paints the skies so bright,
Sandy bears hug the light.
Squirrels dance in tiny shorts,
Beachcombers sing, a daily sport!

Golden rays offer a gentle tease,
Hats fly off in the warm breeze.
Seashells chuckle by the sand,
Laughter spills across the land!

Surfboards tumble in comical grace,
Sticky juice drips down the face.
Ice cream melts in the summer heat,
Sandy snacks, oh what a treat!

As the day turns into night,
Fireworks burst in sheer delight.
Under the stars, let humor blend,
A sun-kissed serenade, never end!

Colorful Rhythms in Paradise

In a land where coconuts sway,
The monkeys dance and play all day.
Bamboo sticks become our drums,
While laughter echoes, and worry numbs.

Rainbow fish swim with flair,
They mock us just by being there.
Flip-flops slapping on the beach,
We strut our stuff, that's how we teach.

Tiki torches light the way,
As we groove without delay.
Mango smoothies, icy chill,
A sip of joy, a sip until.

We're all just sunbaked paradise fools,
Wearing grass skirts, breaking all the rules.
In this dance of warmth and cheer,
Who needs a plan? We're living here!

Lullabies of the Emerald Isle

On sunlit shores, we sing our tune,
With giggling waves beneath the moon.
The seagulls squawk a silly song,
They must think we all belong.

Coconut hats with hibiscus bloom,
Transforming us into instant 'boom.'
We twirl around without a care,
Until our ice cream flies through the air.

Lush palm trees sway, they lean,
Trying to catch the goofy scene.
A crab steals my flip-flop away,
But look at me, I still play!

Underneath the bright blue sky,
Friends and laughter, oh my my!
We'll chase the sun until the night,
With silly hearts that feel so right.

Amber Dances on Warm Sands

When morning sun spills golden rays,
The sandcastles wear silly face displays.
We dive with dolphins, belly flop,
And giggles echo, there's no stop.

Sunbathers flaunt their wobbly flair,
As seagulls giggle, light as air.
A crab moves sideways, looking sly,
It knows my sandwich caught its eye.

Sipping drinks with tiny umbrellas,
We toast our luck with beachside fella's.
While sunburns paint us scarlet hues,
We dance it off, we can't refuse.

The beach ball flies, an airborne treat,
We chase it down with dancing feet.
Surrounded by warmth, we stay and play,
In a sand-drenched, laughter-filled ballet.

Secrets in the Coral Gardens

Beneath the waves where mermaids dwell,
Fish gossip secrets they can't repel.
Coral castles glow in the light,
While sea cucumbers hold an insight.

A turtle grins, thinks it's a race,
But slowly drifts, it's got that grace.
With jellyfish, we all take a sway,
Who knew swimming could feel this way?

Octopuses juggle, such a sight,
We clap along in sheer delight.
In the deep blue, we twirl and spin,
Trying to keep that laughter in.

Stars above blink in surprise,
As we dance deep and touch the skies.
In this silly underwater tale,
We're all fish out of water, but we sail.

Currents of Warmth

In the sun, my ice cream melts,
As seagulls steal the snacks I've dealt.
Flip-flops squeak on sandy shores,
While I dodge waves, my laughter roars.

The waves say hi, then splash my face,
A crab scuttles by, what a funny race!
Laughter erupts as friends fall down,
We're the clowns in this beachy town.

Umbrellas dancing, caught by a breeze,
Chasing cool drinks with utmost ease.
The sun's relentless, but so are we,
Sunburned noses, oh what a spree!

As the day fades, we dance in sync,
A conga line formed – let's share a drink!
Under twilight, we share a jest,
In this warm place, we feel so blessed.

Retreat to Eden

Under palm trees, we sip sweet juice,
Misplaced our map—oh, what's the use?
A parrot squawks, he thinks he's wise,
We laugh till we ache, oh what a surprise.

In hammocks hung too low, we lie,
With a flip of a towel, we might just fly.
Our drinks in hand, we talk and tease,
But that monkey? He's stealing my cheese!

Sun hats big enough to hold a feast,
Yet I forgot lunch – you bring the beast.
We try yoga on the swaying sand,
But I tumble over – must be my hand!

As day turns to night, the laughter soars,
With wonky dances on the sandy floors.
Return to the stars, we giggle and bleed,
Who knew paradise came with such need?

Mirage of Hidden Waters

Oh look, there's a pool, or is it the sea?
I cannonball in, feeling so free.
"Surprise!" yells my friend—where's his suit?
A splashy mess ends in joyous hoot.

Tiny fishes tickle my toes,
And I shout out loud, "Here comes the prose!"
We sip on drinks with umbrellas so bright,
Lemonade battles break out in delight.

The sun wants to steal all our rays,
But we jest and bubble for hours and days.
A wave is coming! And off I go,
What happened next? Well, that's just the show.

As the sun dips down, back we retreat,
To our ice-cream stash, that can't be beat.
In this mirage, we find sweet mirth,
Hidden in waters, what's the true worth?

Whispers of the Beach

The sands are shifting, what's that sound?
Seashells gossip, beneath the ground.
The tide rolls in, with tales to share,
And the wind's chuckle floats through the air.

A surfboard's wobble becomes my fate,
As I tumble and roll, is this my state?
Laughing seagulls join the parade,
In this sandy circus, blushes are made.

Beach balls bouncing, my neighbor can't catch,
A glorious splash gives the day a patch.
Driftwood dances with stories untold,
While coconut drinks chill, oh so bold.

As night blankets all, we gather round,
Under the stars, where joy's unbound.
The whispers linger, while waves celebrate,
In this beachy realm, life's truly first-rate.

Palette of the Sunset

The sun slips down with a wink,
Painting the sky with fruity pink.
Clouds are strawberries, bright and sweet,
While the sun dances, tapping its feet.

Laughter bubbles from the beach,
As seagulls bicker just out of reach.
Surfboards wobble like drunken fools,
In a contest of splashes—the best of schools!

Bikini tops like candy wrappers,
Float on beaches full of giggling clappers.
The horizon giggles, a visual treat,
As sunset wraps us in its fruity sheet.

Glass of coconut, cheers in the air,
With friends all around, without a care.
As the day ends in a party of hues,
We toast to the night, with laughter and ruse.

Harmony of the Rainforest

Under the canopy, a chorus of sound,
Bakery of bananas, they've all come 'round.
Parrots compete, with jokes in their call,
While sloths hang around, with time for them all.

Frogs croak softly, a rhythmic delight,
Setting the mood for a bug-dancing night.
In the shadows, a snake does a twist,
"Hey, who touched my tail?" he swings in a mist!

Monkeys are swinging, their jokes in the air,
Stealing your lunch, just because they dare.
The leaves rustle with giggles and cheer,
As Mother Nature cracks jokes in your ear!

Rain drizzles down like a playful tease,
Turning the ground into a mud-slide breeze.
Wildlife joins in this lively spree,
Celebrating chaos, just wait and see!

Echoes of the Mangrove

In the mangroves, the crabs are kings,
Dancing sideways with fancy things.
A fish splashes, making a point,
"Hey, check my style, I'm the flipping joint!"

Oysters giggle with shells so bright,
While the tide plays tag, a splashy delight.
Egrets strike poses, they're masters of glam,
"Look at me gliding, I'm too cool, man!"

Roots like dancers spread out in grace,
As mudskippers hop, the party's their place.
Each whispering wave has a story to share,
While the sun's golden rays mess up your hair!

Echoes of laughter and splashes galore,
In this watery world, who could ask for more?
Let's toast the tide, cheers to the muck,
In this quirky haven, we've run out of luck!

Kiss of the Ocean's Mist

The mist hugs close like a friendly ghost,
Tickling your nose as it dances boast.
Waves are crafting their whimsical tales,
While surfers flip, like they're out of scale!

Seaweed sways as the rhythm grows loud,
"I'm the best dancer!" it shouts out proud.
The sand giggles under each wandering foot,
While crabs join in with a comical scoot!

Seagulls argue over the best fish fry,
While beach balls soar and kisses fly high.
Shells clamor on beaches with gossip galore,
As the ocean's sweet breath curls to the shore.

At dusk, the horizon wears a tangerine grin,
With nightfall that tickles the cheek of the grin.
In this play of waves, we all find a place,
Where laughter's enchanted, in nature's embrace!

Drink in the Ocean's Colors

The waves are green, like guacamole,
I take a sip, and say, quite slowly,
Is this a beach or a taco stand?
I dance with jellyfish—oh, so grand!

My drink's a shade of sunset red,
With pineapple slices, they dance, they spread!
Even the seaweed waves hello,
I'll drink it all, then ride the flow!

The crabs do the cha-cha by the shore,
In flip-flops, they're ready for more!
With shells as hats, they strut so proud,
At this beach, we're all part of the crowd!

So here's my toast to the ocean's hues,
With coconut cocktails and slippery shoes!
Let's dip our toes in this bubbly spree,
Where laughter flows as wild as the sea!

Horizon's Embrace

The sun dips low, like a silly clown,
It paints the sky in a splotchy gown.
Seagulls giggle, squawking like kids,
While beach balls bounce off unsuspecting lids.

Clouds float by, looking quite confused,
Wishing they brought their sunblock, bruised.
A dolphin does flips, shows off its bling,
While I sip my drink—my new favorite fling!

The sand's so hot, it tickles my feet,
Just like my dance moves—too hard to beat!
With beach parties rocking, we laugh and play,
Until the stars tell us it's the end of the day.

Here in this place where smiles unite,
We share our jokes 'til the morning light.
Let's dream of horizons that tease and roll,
While the ocean sings—what a fun-filled soul!

Heartfelt Horizons

Beneath a palm, I swing and sway,
My cocktail's melting in a sunny display.
The sand's so fine, I make little hills,
With antics so silly, it gives me thrills.

A beach ball bounces, oh what a sight!
As friends take turns in a friendly fight.
Splashing in waves, we create a splash,
The laughter echoes—a joyful crash!

Tanned sunbathers wear shades that match,
While seagulls cry, they're ready to snatch.
The mood is light, like whipped cream fluff,
We cheer and sing, 'This is enough!'

So here's my heart on this sandy ground,
With goofy times, laughter all around.
In this wild embrace of sun and sea,
We find our joy—just you and me!

Colors of the Crescendo

Sprightly hues in the setting light,
Coconuts dancing, oh what a sight!
The sun turns orange, the waves shimmer blue,
As I juggle pineapples—just for you!

The breeze throws confetti, what a grand show,
I trip on a sandcastle (take it slow!).
With laughter erupting from everyone near,
We toast to the ocean, and cheer with a beer!

A crab steals my flip-flop, the little rogue,
I chase down the beach like a bumbling trog.
While shells play their trumpets and seagulls croon,
We dance till the stars peek out, oh so soon.

So here's to the fun in this colorful scene,
Where laughter and joy reign, pure and serene.
In waves of delight, we find our beat,
With every splash, we're moving our feet!

Secrets of the Coral Reef

Beneath the waves, fish go to school,
With lessons taught by a wise old fool.
They dance and twirl, a colorful spree,
In hidden depths where giggles run free.

A crab in a tux, looking quite grand,
Claims regal rights over seaweed land.
He snaps his claws, puts on a show,
But trips on a shell—oh, what a blow!

Starfish play poker, without any stakes,
While dolphin jokes keep everyone awake.
A sea turtle tells tales of a rock,
That glowed like the sun… but it was just a sock!

With laughter echoing in bubbles of air,
The ocean's secrets come with a flair.
So if you dive in where laughter is rife,
You'll find the coral has a comical life.

Driftwood Memories

A piece of driftwood told me a tale,
Of seashells that danced at the end of the trail.
They rolled and they flipped, with not a care,
In a sunbeam's glow, without a single glare.

The seagulls laughed as they played peek-a-boo,
With wobbly waves that said, "Howdy-do!"
And crabs with sunglasses strutted so bold,
Claiming the beach as their stories unfold.

A jellyfish jived in a glow-in-the-dark,
Leading the dance with a zap and a spark.
As the sunset faded, they all joined in,
Turning driftwood dreams into a wild spin.

So gather your pieces from shores far and wide,
And join the driftwood, let humor be your guide.
For memories made where laughter is free,
Are treasures worth more than any deep sea.

Heartbeats in the Tropics

In a hammock swinging, I sip coconut cheer,
While monkeys above shout, "Hey, come over here!"
They throw down their bananas with playful glee,
As if sharing breakfast is just meant to be.

Parrots squawk stories of a pirate's old loot,
With squishy mangos as their favorite fruit.
The rhythm of life beats like a drum,
In a jungle where laughter is always the sum.

A chameleon chuckles, changing from green,
To bright neon hues, what a vivid scene!
He slips on a leaf, with a splash and a grin,
"I blend in just fine, but I'm awkward within!"

As sunbeams giggle through leaves up above,
The air is thick with mischief and love.
With heartbeats a-thrum in this curious place,
The tropics bring joy at an unpredictable pace.

Meadow of Silken Shadows

In a meadow of silk, the daisies prance,
With butterflies flapping, so full of romance.
They sip on sweet nectar, so rich and divine,
But watch out for bees, they'll start to whine!

A grasshopper plays on a fiddle made green,
While crickets join in, creating a scene.
As the sun casts its glow, a funny sight finds,
A snail on a journey, leaving laughter behind.

The clouds drift like marshmallows, soft and light,
While dandelions play hide and seek with delight.
"Catch us if you can!" they tease with a sigh,
As the wind blows them off in a swoosh through the sky.

Laughter and color, life's joyous parade,
In this field full of shadows, adventures are made.
So dance with the flowers, let whimsy be known,
In a meadow where humor has freely grown.

Fragrant Echoes Beneath the Canopy

In the jungle where the monkeys play,
Pineapple dreams dance all day.
Parrots squawk with silly cheer,
While sloths lounge, sipping root beer.

Mangoes giggle, fall from trees,
Chasing lizards in the breeze.
Vines twist up in playful knots,
As the laughter never stops.

Rubbing shoulders with a bee,
Who insists he's royalty.
With pollen crowns and buzzing grace,
He shows us all how to embrace.

By the river, frogs conspire,
Croaking songs to raise the choir.
In this lush and funny place,
Nature's quirks, a cool embrace.

Silk-Skinned Sunsets

Golden hues on rolling waves,
Where seagulls laugh and freedom braves.
Palm trees shake their leafy hair,
Whispering secrets without a care.

A coconut rolls down the sand,
Chasing crabs, oh isn't it grand?
Flip-flops are lost, a funny fight,
As the tide dances into the night.

Sunscreen squirted, splatters fly,
Looks like the beach just said goodbye!
Everyone's smudged, a canvas bright,
Life at sunset becomes the light.

With each laugh and playful splash,
Time slows down as the colors crash.
Golden rays begin to fade,
Yet memories in our hearts are made.

Coconut Kisses and Ocean Waves

Coconuts plop, a sweet surprise,
As waves tickle our toes and ties.
A parrot steals a sip of drink,
With winks and squawks, what do you think?

Surfboards tumble, giggles roar,
Sandy warriors hit the shore.
Flip-flops fly in a playful game,
As laughter rings, we forget our fame.

Seashells whisper their sandy tales,
Of pirate ghosts and windy gales.
With a grin, we each take turns,
Pretending that the ocean learns.

So let the waves crash with delight,
In this beach of goofy sights.
Every splash brings a brand new cheer,
With coconut kisses and good cheer.

Embrace of the Vivid Grotto

In the grotto where colors tease,
A splash of jellyfish makes me freeze.
Sunlight giggles through the rocks,
While shrimps take selfies in their socks.

Coral castles rise up high,
As fish parade by wearing ties.
With each shimmy and every wave,
Even the clams are feeling brave.

A sea turtle grins, so wise and sly,
Winks at the octopus passing by.
There's a crab with a royal crown,
Holding court in a seaweed gown.

As bubbles rise and jokes unfold,
The underwater secrets are bold.
In this grotto of silly grace,
We find laughter's warm embrace.

Rustling Leaves in the Afternoon

Leaves giggle as they sway,
Waving at the sun's bright ray.
A monkey swings and grins wide,
Wondering where his lunch will hide.

A parrot tells a joke so crude,
While on the ground, ants share their food.
Laughter echoes through the trees,
As squirrels dance in playful breeze.

A lizard joins in on the fun,
In search of warmth, he finds the sun.
A chorus of frogs croaks a beat,
As crickets tap their tiny feet.

With every rustle, a chuckle flows,
Nature's comedy in every pose.
The afternoon giggles, oh what a show,
In a realm where joy and mischief grow.

Heartbeats of the Mango Grove

Mangoes tumble, it's quite a sight,
One lands near a goat's delight.
He snorts and leaps, so full of glee,
As others roll down foolishly.

A bird steals fruit, then takes a bow,
"Bravo!" shouts the crowd, oh wow!
The wind tickles, it whispers sweet,
Turning frisbees into treats.

The heartbeat thumps in perfect sync,
Mango juice splashes, they all drink.
In every shade, laughter unrolled,
Stories of silly antics told.

The sun sets low, the grove takes heed,
With giggles shared, it's all we need.
In this sweet spot, joy does grow,
Where hearts align in the mango flow.

Enchanted Waters and Sun-Kissed Shores

Waves curl up, then tumble down,
Tickling toes of a surfer clown.
He takes a fall, but what a splash,
Giggling seashells cheer the crash!

A crab's got moves, a dance routine,
The sun watches, oh, what a scene!
"Let's get crabs to join our game!"
Laughter pops, like bubbles, lame.

Seagulls squawk in a fancy flight,
While sunbathers sunbathe too tight.
A flip-flop flies through the air,
Someone yelps, "Hey! That's not fair!"

The sun-kissed shores echo with cheer,
Where every splash brings lovers near.
In enchanted waters, nothing feels bland,
Just silliness, laughter, and a hand in hand.

Melting Into the Sunset

Shadows stretch as day turns sweet,
A cow licks ice cream off her feet.
The cone's too tall, she's in a fix,
Laughing birds shout, "Try some tricks!"

Colors mix in a funny dance,
Sun melts low, it's a silly trance.
A cat chases hues with a pout,
Crepuscular pranks, there's no doubt.

Flip-flops squeak on the boardwalk's edge,
While folks make bets by the hedge.
"Who can twirl for this last bite?"
Laughter erupts, what a delight!

As night descends on joy's parade,
Chasing sunsets that never fade.
With smiles painted on every face,
Life melts sweetly into grace.

Waves' Gentle Lullaby

The sea brings giggles, not a frown,
As turtles wear hats, flip upside down.
A crab in a snout whispers some jokes,
While fish in tuxedos chat with the folks.

The waves dance lightly, no need to rush,
Splashing with laughter, creating a hush.
Jellyfish bob like balloons in the air,
While seagulls swoop down, with time to spare.

Beneath the sun's grin, the beach throws a show,
With sandcastles crumbling, their towers in tow.
Each grain a story, a giggling spree,
Where jelly and sand make a quirky decree.

Let's join the ruckus, the waves call us near,
We'll dance with the dolphins, release all our cheer.
So pack up your worries, the sea's full of glee,
In this wave of laughter, let's just be free!

Colors of the Lagoon

In a lagoon where parrotfish play,
Rainbow hues burst forth in a lively display.
The squawking macaws, with flair and style,
Paint everything bright, they'll make you smile.

Lemons and limes float, a fruit fest anew,
As otters wear sunglasses, quite the view!
They sip on coconut drinks, so divine,
While the wind hums along, keeping perfect time.

A shark with a bow tie checks his reflection,
Ready to dance in a grand pool perfection.
The water's an artist, with splashes and streams,
Composing a symphony of vibrant dreams.

So join the parade, come dip your toes,
In this canvas of laughter, where fun always flows.
With colors enchanting, our spirits will soar,
In the heart of the lagoon, who could ask for more?

Sunlit Escape

The sun giggles bright, as it rises high,
Inviting all swimmers, 'Come on, let's fly!'
Beach balls go bouncing, like stars that gleam,
While sunburned tourists are caught in a beam.

Flip-flops are singing a tap-tap-tune,
As seagulls pirouette, under the moon.
With sand in our toes and laughter in air,
We'll chase down the sunsets without a care.

Pineapples wear shades, while waves do a dance,
Encouraging surfers to give it a chance.
A crab wears a tie, quite dapper and neat,
As the ocean keeps time, tapping its beat.

Let's race through the surf, let kindness outshine,
With giggles and splashes, this moment is mine.
In a sunlit escape, fun is our guide,
In the warmth of the beach, let's laugh side by side!

Embrace of the Shoreline

The shoreline giggles as beach balls collide,
While flip-flops do the cha-cha, full of pride.
A squirrel with a surfboard, ready for fun,
Takes a leap off the sand, with a splash—he's won!

Seashells are whispering secrets galore,
As crabs wear sunglasses and dance on the shore.
The tide rolls in, like a playful kid,
Leaving footprints of laughter, where moments are hid.

A dolphin does flips, with a wink and a grin,
While beachgoers cheer—let the fun begin!
Every wave tells tales, of splashes and games,
As the sun sets all pink, igniting our flames.

Let's treasure the moments, with smiles that seep,
In the embrace of the shoreline, our joy runs deep.
With fun in the air, let's make memories bright,
Here by the waves, we'll dance into the night!

Islands of Serenity

On shores where seagulls squawk and dive,
A crab in a tuxedo feels so alive.
He waltzes on sand with grace so fine,
While tourists chuckle and sip their wine.

A parrot squawks, "You lost your hat!"
As folks ignore that silly cat.
They chase coconuts rolling down,
Each trip revealing a face of a clown.

Flip-flops flapping like happy toes,
Beach volleyball turns to comedy shows.
With every trip and trip they find,
A limbo contest that leaves them blind.

The sun dips low, casting shadows wide,
As beachgoers giggle and take a ride.
In this haven of laughter and fun,
Life feels like a never-ending run.

Whispering Palms

Beneath the palms the whispers grow,
"Did you hear the one about the crow?"
It danced on a branch with spunk and flair,
Just to impress a nearby hare.

Two turtles race for a snack so sweet,
One's on a diet, still feels the heat.
While locals laugh at their slow-motion,
Merging humor with all the ocean.

The coconuts giggle as they fall,
Bouncing off heads, oh, what a ball!
Pineapples join in, with hats askew,
Fruit salad forming, a wacky view.

As the breeze carries tales from the shore,
Adventures beckon and spirits soar.
With laughter echoing far and near,
Whispering palms hold the joy we hear.

Lush Breeze Reveries

In the lush greens where critters prance,
A frog in sunglasses starts his dance.
With every leap and boisterous croak,
The jungle bursts into laughter's cloak.

A monkey swings, not quite aware,
Of the vines that tangle in its hair.
With a swing and a hop, it zooms on by,
While tourists snap pics, suppressing a sigh.

Coconuts roll like bowling balls,
And a toucan's riddle just defies all.
"Why did the fish join the comedy show?
To find the humor in the flow!"

A hammock sways with a gentle sway,
As sleepyheads nap their afternoon away.
Laughter mixes with the rustling leaves,
In this paradise where joy never leaves.

Sunset Melodies

As the sun dips low, the sky turns gold,
An octopus strums, adventurous and bold.
With eight arms jiving to a tune so fine,
It steals the show, making fish entwine.

A dolphin joins, leaping in sync,
With a splash and a wink, non-stop, I think!
The beachgoers dance, they shake and sway,
In this melody where worries fray.

"Why did the sunset break into song?"
It wanted to shine where shadows belong.
With every note, they clap and cheer,
Echoing joy through the atmosphere.

The night gently falls, stars start to peep,
As laughter lingers, it's time to leap.
In this vibrant haven, wild and free,
The sunset serenades, just wait and see.

Ocean's Warm Caress

The ocean waves come crashing in,
Like playful dolphins trying to win.
Flip-flops flying, laughter rings,
As sandcastles sway on seaweed swings.

Beach chairs tipped, a seagull's feast,
A sandwich snatched, our joy increased.
Crab legs waltz, they dance a jig,
While sunburned folks do the limbo dig.

Pineapple drinks served with a smile,
Sunhat tilted, it's beachy style.
We're all just kids with grown-up dreams,
Chasing waves and ice cream streams.

As twilight falls, the colors gleam,
We laugh and shout, "This place is a dream!"
The ocean's warmth, a goofy song,
In salty air, we all belong.

Exotic Dreams Under Starlight

Under the stars, we sip coconut,
Imagining adventures in this cute rut.
A gecko serenades with glee,
And the moon winks, just for me.

A hammock sways, like a gentle tease,
Coconut crabs scurry with ease.
Mango salsa spills on my lap,
As I battle bugs for a quick nap.

Driftwood crafts with a flair of fun,
Making treasures in the setting sun.
With jellyfish glowing, it's quite the sight,
We stumble and laugh in the soft moonlight.

In dreams of paradise, we all float,
As sea turtles march, their funny gloat.
Adventure awaits beneath the sky,
With a wink and a grin, let's fly high!

Dance of the Hibiscus

Hibiscus blooms with a sassy sway,
Dancing gently in the sun's warm ray.
Butterflies flutter, a vivid sight,
While the lizards join in with delight!

A calypso band plays tunes so sweet,
As tourists shuffle to the lively beat.
Limbo sticks stand, a challenge ablaze,
Who knew bending would earn us praise?

A parrot squawks, "Aloha, my friend!"
His comedy act never seems to end.
In a floral shirt, oh what a scene,
Mixing laughter with a drink so green.

At sundown, we cheer, the day's a hit,
With cheeky banter and a little wit.
Under palm trees swaying free,
We dance and laugh, just you and me!

Serenade of the Sea

The sea sings songs of laughter and cheer,
With clams that giggle and dolphins near.
A squid in a hat does a silly jig,
While crabs in tuxes boast and dig.

The tide rolls in, a cheeky friend,
Wetting our toes, oh how it bends.
A beach ball bounces, an aerial stunt,
As kids run wild on their beachy hunt.

With every wave, a splashy joke,
Our sandcastle dreams, the ocean's cloak.
Seashells whisper, secrets of glee,
In this joyful, lively jubilee.

As night sets in, the stars all bright,
We swap our tales under the light.
With giggles and grins, we sing along,
In the serenade of where we belong.

Nectar of Celestial Isle

On the beach, the fruit has grown,
Pineapples sing in a juicy tone.
Coconuts dance, they roll and bob,
While crabs strut like they're in a mob.

Parrots gossip, full of cheer,
Squawking secrets in our ear.
Sunburned tourists trying to tan,
Slip on their flip-flops, oh what a plan!

Sunset cocktails spill a bit,
Lime juice garnish, oh, what a hit!
Sandy toes and a goofy grin,
In this isle, let the fun begin!

With a grin, I chase a kite,
Only to trip—oh, what a sight!
Laughter echoes, waves create,
Joy flows freely; isn't life great?

Pinks and Golds of Dusk

The sky's a canvas, paints so bright,
Chickens roam, they think they might.
In rickety boats, we set afloat,
While finding fish that just won't gloat.

The sun dips low, casting a blush,
As cows join in, they seem to rush.
They moo in sync with the tides that sway,
Reminding us, it's a funny day!

The mangoes plop, and oh the splats,
As seagulls plot their sneaky chats.
Drawn in by dusk, with giggles shared,
Life's simple joys, how none are spared!

Stars peek out, with a wink and nod,
A crab just marched; how slight, how odd.
Under the laughter, moonlight beams,
We find silly fun in our wild dreams.

Lullaby of the Lagoon

A lullaby hums from the sleepy waves,
While fishes hide in their sandy caves.
Turtles twirl in a gentle race,
Swaying along with a comical grace.

A hammock swings on a coconut breeze,
As my drink spills—oh, if you please!
With a splash, the parrot laughs so loud,
Making fish wobble under the cloud.

My flip-flop slips, and an octopus grins,
It perfects my dance as the party begins!
Under the palms, we twirl and sway,
An awkward ballet in the sun's soft ray.

So here we lie, in chaos we bask,
Trading silly jokes, no need to ask.
The lagoon hums with laughter and fun,
In this whimsical land, we're never done!

Passage through Paradise

With a snorkel, I dive in the froth,
Only to find a fish doing a swath!
It darts with glee, in colors so bright,
As I splash water in sheer delight.

A boat sails by, with a jolly crew,
They serenade waves and a coconut too!
We join their tune—what a silly sight,
Dancing with dolphins till the moon is white.

Now a crab steals my sandwich with finesse,
As I stand aghast, I must confess!
With laughter in my heart, I toss him bread,
He scuttles away, "Thanks!" he seems to said!

Starlit whispers coat the night sky,
With a twist and twirl, my worries fly.
In this passage, all joy is served,
Life's a giggle ride—whoever observed?

The Sweet Scent of Paradise

In a garden where the fruits do dance,
A pineapple wore a silly pants.
Coconuts chuckled on the vine,
While mangoes schemed a fruit punch line.

Papayas giggled in the hot sun's glow,
Saying, "We're ripe, come see the show!"
Bananas pitched a peel-filled game,
Oh, the joy of tropical fame!

Limes rolled over with a zesty cheer,
"Sour faces won't be welcome here!"
Watermelons laughed in stripes of green,
In this paradise, all is seen.

So grab a drink, let's dance and sway,
The fruit bowl sings, come join the fray!
Under the sun, where spirits collide,
Life is a party, come take a ride!

Ocean's Embrace at Dusk

The waves tease sand, a frothy jest,
They tickle toes, at their playful best.
Seagulls squawk in a cheeky choir,
As surfers claim, "Mornings are dire!"

Shells gossip as they bask in hues,
Whispers of clams, with ocean news.
A crab pranced by, in a tiny hat,
"I'm the sea's fashion, fancy that!"

The moon peeks out, with a wink, oh dear,
Laughing at fish with salty beer.
Stars twinkle bright on the ocean's crest,
A wave of giggles, life is a fest!

So join the tide, let laughter flow,
Ride the swell and let the good times grow.
At dusk, the ocean wears a bright grin,
A call to play, let the fun begin!

Moonlit Shadows on the Beach

The moon pranced down with a silvery beam,
Painting the sand like a starlit dream.
Footprints danced upon the shore's bright face,
As crabs held a race at an awkward pace.

A turtle giggled, "I can't be fast!"
Flapping his flippers, he came in last.
Stars shimmered down, a disco ball,
While shadows of palm trees began to sprawl.

Seashells chatted with a sprinkle of sand,
"Is it time for karaoke? Join our band!"
The night filled with laughter, it echoed near,
As the ocean waved, "Let's give a cheer!"

So twirl and spin 'neath the moonlit sky,
With shadows of joy that flutter and fly.
Under the glow, let your heart be free,
This magical night is just for me!

Lively Currents of Joy

In a river woven like a joyful tune,
Where fish jump high beneath the moon.
Croaking frogs join in a splashing play,
"Leap if you can, we can rhyme all day!"

A water snake whispers with a wink,
"Don't mind the splash, just join the drink!"
While turtles bob like tiny boats,
In currents filled with laughter floats.

The lilies flail in a leafy dance,
"Come have a whirl, take a chance!"
Dragonflies giggle, strutting bright,
This lively stream's a pure delight!

So paddle on through this joyful mess,
In a world where fun is never less.
With currents of glee forever sway,
Join the river, come laugh and play!

Heirlooms of Coral

In the sea, a crab wears bling,
As fish parade in a conga ring.
Octopus in shoes, a fashion spree,
Sipping coconut milk, what a sight to see!

Jellyfish dance, glowing like stars,
While seagulls squawk about their cars.
Anemones giggle, tickled by waves,
Who knew the ocean could host such braves?

Coral castles hold a vibrant flay,
Where sea turtles munch on buffet all day.
Underwater laughter fills the reef,
Silly sea life brings us such relief.

So, cheers to the sea with laughs untold,
Where every fin has a tale of gold.
It's a splashy world where humor prevails,
In depths of coral, joy never fails!

Flames of Hibiscus

Hibiscus hats align on heads,
While lizards share jokes in comfy beds.
Sunshine smiles as laughter rings,
While parrots trade their silly flings.

Bumblebees buzz, wearing shades,
While kittens chase their shady glades.
A flamingo slips, strikes a pose,
As laughter erupts and no one knows.

Tropical drinks with silly straws,
Serve as tonic for laughter's cause.
Balloons floating in vibrant display,
A circus of life, where jokers play.

So let your giggles rise and swell,
In fiery blooms, all's well, all's well.
A garden of chuckles, blooms ever bright,
In petals of joy, let's dance tonight!

Eternal Summer's Embrace

Sandy toes in flip-flop flair,
As coconut drinks fly through the air.
A sunburned crab strikes a dizzy pose,
With shades on his pinchers, that's how it goes.

Surfers wipe out, splash like a splash,
Chasing waves in a comical dash.
Seashells whisper jokes from the tide,
While tourists attempt to go for a ride.

Kite-flying fish in a brilliant blue,
Having a contest on who's the best crew.
Mangoes bounce under a sky so bright,
As laughter erupts in the sheer delight.

With each sunset, mischief takes flight,
Unicorns dance in the fading light.
Here's to the sun—let the giggles remain,
In the warmth of the waves, we'll never feel pain!

Cascading Palm Shadows

Beneath tall palms, shadows do play,
Cockatoos gossip about their day.
Swaying branches hold a cane to tease,
While monkeys swing with infinite ease.

Tropical breeze tickles the vines,
As lizards sip lemonade with limes.
Falling coconuts land with a thud,
Leaving everyone laughing in the mud.

Crabs and clams hold a grand debate,
Over who makes the most scrumptious plate.
A boat drifts by with a party of cheer,
And a parrot squawks, "More fun over here!"

So let's lounge in this shade divine,
With laughter and snacks, and sips of wine.
In the palms of summer, joy takes its claim,
In the shadows of fun, we're all the same!

Sandcastles of Desire

A bucket and a spade in hand,
We build our dreams in golden sand.
Mighty towers, oh so grand,
Until the tide erases our land.

Seagulls laughing as they dive,
Swooping low, they seem alive.
Our castles fall, but still we strive,
For next time, we'll make them thrive!

With seashells as our treasure trove,
We daydream as the waves all rove.
But truth be told, we can't approve,
When a dog comes by and makes his move!

So here's to laughter on the shore,
With grainy cheeks and sandy lore.
We'll build again forevermore,
Until we tire—let's hit the store!

Lore of the Warm Winds

The wind whispers tales of glee,
Of dancing hips and coconut tea.
Laughter floats like a bumblebee,
In the breeze, oh so carefree!

With hula moves and big sun hats,
A conga line of clumsy cats.
They zigzag by, oh what of that?
Our windblown hair a funny stat!

Banana peels slip underfoot,
As we attempt a stylish hoot.
The sandy floor, our natural loot,
We laugh out loud in playful pursuit!

So dance with me, let worries cease,
In this warm breeze, we find our peace.
With giggles shared, may joy increase,
And through the chaos, love's release!

Spirals of Palm Fronds

Palm fronds sway like funky hair,
In a cha-cha dance, with flair to spare.
We join the rhythm, without a care,
As coconuts drop here and there!

The sun beats down, a golden ray,
We sweat a lot; come on, let's play!
But who needs towels when sunshine's sway,
Dries us off in a silly way?

With capes made from colorful mats,
We pose like super-heroes, just like that.
A beach ball bounces, here and that,
As laughter reigns, our favorite chat!

So under palms where shadows cast,
We'll wear our smiles and have a blast.
With every wave that swirls so fast,
We treasure moments that ever last.

Elysium of the Earth

In paradise, we find a feast,
With fruity drinks, not just a tease.
Umbrellas rainbowed, oh, what a beast,
We sip away, our worries ceased!

The laughter echoes through the sky,
As turtles wear their sunglasses high.
With each wild tale and goofy sigh,
We find ourselves in joyful pie!

Jumping waves and doing flips,
Like fish out of the water—oops, our slips!
With noodle fights and bubble trips,
We float along on laughter's ships!

So raise your glass to sunny days,
Where every sunset paints a blaze.
In this land where cheer always stays,
The essence of life in funny ways!

Island Moonsong

Under the moon, coconuts sway,
Bouncing crabs dance, with much to say.
A parrot squawks, in feathered delight,
While locals strum on ukuleles each night.

Sandy toes tickle, as laughter flies,
Fish tell jokes, while the sea turtle sighs.
A chorus of frogs join in the tune,
As starfish groan about their sore afternoon.

Mermaids giggle, with shells in their hair,
Playing snap with a dolphin, a stylish affair.
The seaweed shakes, in a limbo contest,
As sandy beach boys show off their best.

So grab your drink, with a colorful straw,
Join the crabs in their hemp-woven law.
Tonight's the night for silly fun,
With laughter rolling like waves from the sun.

Enchanted Shores

On the shores where the pineapples grow,
Pebbles giggle, as they skitter low.
A beach ball sails, like a bird in the air,
While sunscreen warriors fight the sun's daring glare.

Hula dancers spin, with grass skirts afloat,
A hippo in shades, steals the lifeguard's boat.
Tunes from a conch shell, a symphony rare,
And slapstick slip-ups, as friends tumble and share.

Coconuts roll, like jokes from a clown,
While the jellyfish flaunt, dressing up in their gown.
Seagulls swoop low, for a snack on the run,
As laughter erupts like the waves, just for fun.

So gather your friends, on this magical sand,
With antics and fun, let's all take a stand.
Under the sun, with a grin ear to ear,
Every moment here, brings us laughter and cheer.

Wildflower Dreams

In a field where daisies do play,
Bumblebees buzz, in a silly ballet.
With butterflies laughing, they swirl and sway,
As daisies declare, it's a flowerful day!

Tulips try to keep up, while roses don hats,
Sunflowers chat, with the playful cats.
Amidst the clovers, a rabbit in pants,
Winks at the daisies, "Let's start a dance!"

Breezes play tricks, tickling the grass,
As wildflowers shout, "Look at us sass!"
A squirrel joins in, with nuts on parade,
While crickets conduct an orchestra made.

So let's lay here, with laughter unfurled,
As nature hums sweet tunes of this quirky world.
With petals a-flutter and joy in the stream,
We're wrapped in the magic of wildflower dreams.

Sailboats Salute the Stars

On a night when the sailboats glide,
The captain's a cat, and the crew's got pride.
Stars giggle in awe, as they twinkle bright,
While dolphins debate, who jumps the highest tonight.

With popcorn clouds and a sprinkle of fun,
The moon throws a party, the night has begun.
Pirates toast toasties, with jellyfish cheer,
As mermaids and sailors swap tales in good beer.

The wind plays a tune on the sails of delight,
As gulls join the chorus, taking flight.
With treasure maps drawn on the back of a napkin,
The laughter rolls on, as the fun starts to happen.

So raise your glass at the harbor's embrace,
To the mischief and magic, we all now face.
With stars in our eyes and joy in our hearts,
Adventure awaits, as the real fun starts!

Vibrance of the Tropic Hearts

In a hammock swaying high,
Laughing at clouds passing by,
Giant fruits with eyes that wink,
They giggle as they start to sink.

Sandy toes and coconut drinks,
Dancing fish give playful blinks,
A parrot squawks with glee and sass,
Stealing my sun hat—what a lass!

Breezes blow with a cheeky grin,
Palm trees sway as if to spin,
A crab in shades, walks by with flair,
I've lost my shoes, but I don't care!

Sunset paints with crayons bright,
Colorful cocktails take to flight,
Each sip brings more giggles near,
Life here is a comedy, my dear!

Dames de la Mer

Seashells gossip on the shore,
Mermaids laughing, begging for more,
Waves jump up with silly grace,
Clams dance in a rhythmic race.

Their hair a rainbow, wild and free,
Shell necklaces, oh so fancy,
One tells jokes, and all reply,
'What's a fish's favorite tie?'

Umbrella drinks spill on the sand,
Funny hats drawn by hand,
Octopus juggling with finesse,
Their laughter, a joyful mess!

Crabs in suits hold court so proud,
In this land, they laugh out loud,
As the sun dips below the sea,
Funny tales, just you and me!

Beneath the Baobab

Beneath the tree, oh what a sight,
Fruits that giggle in the night,
A sloth with sunglasses, chilling slow,
Claims he's the fastest in the show.

Chameleons play hide and seek,
Changing colors, quite unique,
A frog with jokes, croaks his punchline,
Where is the water? Just fine wine!

Bugs in disco suits all sway,
Chaotic dancing on display,
A grasshopper sings like a star,
His mic—a twig, oh how bizarre!

As night unfolds, they tell their tales,
Of silly dreams and epic fails,
Laughter echoes, fills the air,
In this paradise, jokes to share!

Chasing Paradise's Glow

Roaming through the fields so bright,
Chasing critters left and right,
A monkey wearing socks so loud,
Doing flips—he's quite the crowd!

Coconuts in perfect lines,
Humming tunes to sunny rhymes,
A toucan paints the sky with cheer,
Scribbling doodles, oh so dear.

Sunshine laughing on my face,
Flowers dancing with such grace,
A lizard posing for the show,
Says he's ready for a glow!

Every step, a giggle here,
In this slice where joy is near,
Life is a riot, come and play,
Let's chase the laughter—every day!

www.ingramcontent.com/pod-product-compliance
Lightning Source LLC
Chambersburg PA
CBHW072117070526
44585CB00016B/1479